JUST ONE...

THE DATING DILEMMA

WORDS OF WISDOM
BOOK ONE

GRACIE LYNNE

ISBN: 979-8-9861539-4-0 (print)

ISBN: 979-8-9861539-3-3 (ebook)

Dedicated to everyone who has encountered the dilemma of dating in this wonderful and crazy world.

FOREWORD

This devotional is taken from a blog that I started in 2013. During that time in my life I had an active dating life.

I learned so many lessons of love during that time and I would like to humbly share these words of wisdom with you. I hope you are inspired by these writings and I truly hope you find your forever love.

THE MESS OF ME...

❧

To be honest, I was a mess. I was a single mother, raising three children, working in a career which I hated, and I could not find Mr. Right.

I was searching for Mr. Right through online dating. If I dated one man and he didn't work out, there were plenty more fish in the ocean. All I had to do was cast my line and find another one. Occasionally, I would get my heart broken, but instead of going to my heavenly Father and seeking to heal my broken heart, I merely put my line back in the ocean and reeled in another man.

One piece of advice: *You can't mend a broken heart by allowing it to be broken again any more than you can cure a disease by contracting another illness.*

Most of the men I dated wanted one thing, and that was sex. The problem I had with that desire was my belief system. I was a Christian, and I was not supposed to have sex outside of marriage. I would tell them I was Christian, but the men I dated did not respect this conviction and would keep pressuring me.

I allowed my own convictions to be disrespected so much that premarital sex was no big thing. I mean, everyone was doing it. Most of the men I dated were "Christian" and they were doing it, so what was so wrong about it?

Then I had a birthday. I turned 50. During this year, I analyzed my life and realized several things.

The first thing I did was give thanks. I gave thanks for my children. I reveled in my role as a single mother. I loved my kids to the moon and back, and they were turning out to be such marvelous young adults. I was so grateful to God for the privilege of being allowed to nurture such wonderful individuals.

The second aspect of my life was my career. I was a home health nurse and while raising three children as a single mother, this job was perfect. I could set my own work schedule and could also work in another part-time gig as a consultant. This allowed me to prioritize my children's schedule over my work routine.

However, God had called me to be a Christian author thirteen years prior, and I came to hate doing anything other than what God had called me to do. Because of this, I needed to work on finishing my first novel and transition out of nursing.

There was one more deficit in my life. I was lacking a second husband. My first marriage had not worked out, but I couldn't have asked for a better co-parent for my children. My ex-husband was a very present father, and I will always honor him for that.

However, I was still single. I don't like being single. I wanted a husband. I knew I had been going about this in the wrong way. I was not abiding by God's commandments.

So, I asked God, "What is the big deal about premarital sex?" I had hardened my heart to the point where sexual intimacy did not open the door to love. I had become a serial dater. I still had a figure which could elicit desire, so why not give the men what they wanted?

That is when God told me His story. Which delivered my heart from sexual immorality and tenderly led me on the path of true love. I hope you read on and allow me to share the story of God's love. This moment in time resonates as the most cherished and loving time of my life. At this moment, I was asking God to justify his commandment for sexual purity.

What right did I have to ask him this?

I had no right. I was broken; I was dirty with sin; I was a hypocrite. I would go to church, pretending to be a good Christian, and then be anything but a Christian when dating.

So, at this moment, God had every right to thunder his judgement, exact his wrath and condemn me. He had absolutely every right to disown me. Yet... he did none of that.

He approached me with the tender love of a Father whose heart had been broken many times by me, his cherished daughter. For I, by my actions, had continually chosen to love his adversary rather than him.

When I asked him "what was wrong about premarital sex, I received His story...

"Let's go back to the garden of Eden. Where it all started. When I made Adam and Eve, they were my delight. We used to walk in the garden and talk about everything. We had so much fun, and those walks were the highlight of my day. They would marvel at the beauty of my creation, and I felt so much love for them and from them.

Our relationship was symbolic. When I was with them, it was like the trinity. Three in one and one in three. We used to laugh about this and chant a rhyme. 'Three in one and one in three. I love you and you love me.'

I was so eager every day to see their faces until one evening...

As the cool breezes were dancing across the tender petals of the flowers of paradise, I was on a stroll, looking for my two loves. Just to think of that evening brings tears to my eyes. I looked for them and could not find them. Every day until this day, they would come running into my open arms and I would embrace them with my love.

Where were they now? They didn't, no, they couldn't have. Oh, I hope they didn't eat from the tree of knowledge.

My heart sank. How could the two whom I created, those which I loved, do the one thing which I commanded them not to do? Surely, they did not disobey me.

Yet they were hiding. Why would they hide from my love? I called for Adam, "Where are you?"

A sinking feeling of dread catching my breath. The breath, which I had breathed into this man whom I had created.

From the depths of darkness, Adam replied, "I heard you walking in the garden, so I hid. I was afraid because I was naked."

Anger swelled within my being. "Who revealed to you that you were naked?" I thundered with rage. "Have you dared eat from the tree which I commanded you not to eat from?"

"It was the woman you gave me who gave me the fruit, and I ate it." Adam replied.

I saw no remorse. First, he hides, then he blames the woman and me. Who is this man who I created and loved? I see nothing of the love we shared. He is like a stranger.

Eve stood beside him in defiance of my love. I fell to my knees, crying out in despair. "What have you done?" I screamed out, trembling with despair, facing the woman.

"The serpent deceived me. That's why I ate it." Eve replied, as if to diminish her complicity in this disobedient act.

Once again, there was no remorse, rather a justification of their sin in blaming each other or the serpent. No humility or repentance. Pride had become their covering.

I had to banish them from my garden. If I didn't, they may have eaten from the tree of life and be condemned to live forever in this state of separation from me. I loved them enough to know I wanted more for them than this.

Before they left, I made them clothes. I sacrificed an animal and sewed the skin of this animal together to fashion a covering for their shame. This would be the first of many animals slain for the guilt of man. Until my sweet Son, my most precious lamb, would sacrifice his very life for the sin of humanity.

When they left, I was so alone. I missed the intimacy we had. Adam had Eve and Eve had Adam, but who did I have to love? I wanted to be invited into their intimacy. This is why marriage was created.

The intimacy of sex is such a wonderful act of love. One which I created for humanity to allow procreation and the establishment of families. Symbolically it represents unity and intimacy like I had with Adam and Eve. But *with anything sacred, it demands protection, a covenant agreement of marriage is necessary for the blessing of my protection.*

Adam and Eve betrayed me with their disobedience. I yearn for an invitation to be invited back in and when you have sex outside of marriage; it breaks my heart. I want to be a part of your love, but I want a commitment and covenant between you, your spouse, and me. I want this not only for me, but to protect you and your heart. I desire this because of my love for you."

When I heard this story, it devastated me. I didn't realize my behavior was breaking the heart of God. My spirit crumbled in remorse, and I asked for forgiveness. I told God I loved him, and I didn't want to break his heart anymore.

Then I did the unthinkable. I asked him to take the desire for premarital sex away from me and, in an instant; I was delivered from my mess.

JUST ONE...

I was driving back from Kentucky. I had gone there to view Noah's Ark, and I was hungry. I had a gift card for a certain restaurant, so I stopped in for lunch.

When I entered the lobby, I said I needed a table for one.

The hostess said, "Just one?"

I said, "Yes, just one."

She kept asking me if I was single, which I kept affirming I was. Then she sat me in the most undesirable booth in the whole restaurant. The booth by the kitchen.

I am not one to complain, so I sat there and had the sweetest server waiting on me. He was worth sitting by the kitchen, but it unnerved me a little to be so disregarded because I was "just one."

Although that experience was irritating. I have been single for twenty-five years and I am content. I am devoted to God, who I believe has called me to place Him first in my life. As Paul says in

I Corinthians 7:6-8, (6)

"I say this as a concession: not as a command. (7) But I wish everyone were single, just as I am. Yet each person has a special gift from God, one kind or another.

6

(8) So, I say to those who aren't married and to widows-it's better to stay unmarried just as I am."

When you are single, there is so much freedom to follow God on your journey through life. As much as I would like to be married to the right man, I refuse to be distracted by men whom I know are not God's plan for my life. This allows me to revolve every day around my Lord and savior.

Sometimes I wish I had a husband, but those are the times when I ask God to help me through whatever difficulty I am dealing with, and He has not disappointed me.

Psalms 4:3 Know that the LORD has set apart his faithful servant for himself; the LORD hears when I call to him. (NIV)

CAN you list ten things about being single that you are grateful for?

HOW DO you use this time of solitude to glorify God and serve Him?

DOMESTIC VIOLENCE

I have experience with domestic violence. The first angry man I dated in college. After dating for several months, he held me at gunpoint and threatened to either kill me or rape me. The SWAT team busted in the door before he could do either.

A neighbor in the apartment complex had done the right thing when she heard me screaming. She notified the police.

In another instance of domestic violence, a man choked me when he became angry. I did not call the police. I should have. I do not know if he would have been arrested or not. But that may have discouraged him from further violent acts.

This same man knocked the mirror off my car in a rage. I filed charges against him but dropped the charges when he agreed to have the mirror replaced. It sickens me to think that I filed charges regarding my car, but failed to file charges for my well-being.

The third was a man I dated for two-and-a-half years. He was an alcoholic and although he did not beat me; I was savvy enough to know that he had the characteristics of someone who would use domestic violence if I stayed longer.

Last night I heard the story of another victim of domestic violence. She had been married to her husband for 24 years and had suffered abuse from him. She did not call the police. Now, they are getting divorced. She is making allegations of domestic violence. Without a police report, those allegations may not hold up in divorce court.

Woman, if a man lays a hand on you in anger, violence, or frustration, it is HIS problem NOT yours! Call the police. It is important to have it documented. Get out of the relationship and go to a safe place.

The number for the National Domestic Violence hotline is 1-800-799-7233.

In my experience, the man usually blames the woman for his anger and physical abuse. In no way is a woman responsible for domestic violence. If you do not protect yourself, you may not be able to protect your children, and children deserve a mother who demands protection.

PROVERBS 22:24 Don't make friends with an angry person, and don't be a companion of a hot-tempered one, (CSB)

HAVE you allowed yourself to be abused by someone else?

ARE you currently in an abusive situation?

IF SO, why are you staying in that relationship?

DO YOU DITCH YOUR KIDS FOR A DATE?

Raising three young children and working thirty-two hours on the weekends left little time for a social life. I was attending church with a single group when I was newly divorced, and I had my share of invitations to go out on dates.

I had one standing rule for those men. If they wanted to see me when I had the children, they could guess again. It would not happen. I dated, but always worked it around my children's schedule and when they would be at their father's house.

I had a terrific babysitter; she was about thirty-five miles from my house. Even if she had been next door, I wouldn't have used her to go on a date.

I analyzed what had gone into this decision. I realized as hard as it was to be a single mom, I truly enjoyed my children. The dates, well... not so much.

So, when one of my guy friends from church called me and asked me to lunch one day when my youngest son was home, I said, "No, I don't ditch my kids for a date." That became my motto for that time in my life.

Looking back, I don't miss the men whom I dated or who wanted to date me. If my kids were estranged from me or if anything tragic happened to them while I had been on a date, I would miss them like crazy. I think I made the right decision.

Psalm 127:3 Children are a gift from the LORD; they are a reward from him. (NLT)

HOW IMPORTANT IS DATING to you?

ARE your children second place to your dating, or have you achieved a wonderful balance of both?

DO you treat your children as if they are a gift from God? If not, write down some ways you can change and show your children that they are cherished.

SHOULD YOU RECONCILE WITH SOMEONE WHO HAS ASKED YOUR FORGIVENESS?

$\mathcal{SO}$

This was a topic I saw posted on a Christian Writer's blog. It was a thought-provoking question.

I was wrestling with this in my personal life. An ex-boyfriend was begging for forgiveness and reconciliation. I had changed my phone number, blocked him from my email, and now he had resorted to sending me letters, cards and dropping off food and gifts on my front porch.

Surely, I should reconcile with this man. Right?

I was not at peace when I thought of reconciliation with this man. I was finally living my life and enjoying it. How dare he disturb my joy?

He said God had pointed out what he should ask forgiveness for. I found his pleas for forgiveness self-serving. Most of them revolved around the times he had pushed me away when I tried to show him affection.

I endured the cards for a week, then I put "Return to Sender" on the front and "STOP CONTACTING ME–we are over," on the back. That card went back in the mailbox.

I went out to the mailbox the next afternoon because I felt bad. I didn't want to hurt him. The letter was gone. It had been sent. I would have to deal with my guilt.

The next morning, I was still battling the guilt, and I started praying over the situation. I received a revelation from God. He hadn't asked forgiveness for what God would want me to forgive him for.

The items he would have asked forgiveness for if he was truly hearing from God would have been:

#1 Forgiveness for encouraging me to sin by having premarital sex. I had asked him several times to not pressure me to do that. The pressure continued.

#2 Forgiveness for disrespecting my intelligence and my worth as a human and for treating me as if I was a sex object.

#3 Forgiveness for lying to me on several fronts.

I don't know who he heard, or if he was just making it all up. I doubt he heard God. God does not speak through the Holy Spirit in contrast to what is written in His word.

Once I received wisdom from God, I let go of the guilt. I realized I had chosen the right response. Instead of reconciling with someone who would lead me back into sin, I drew closer to God by walking away from reconciliation.

Deuteronomy 5:33 Follow the whole instruction the Lord your God has commanded you, so that you may live, prosper, and have a long life in the land you will possess. (CSB)

HAS THERE BEEN someone who is trying to reconcile with you?

ON WHAT GROUNDS should you consider reconciliation?

SHOULD YOU BETRAY YOURSELF
IN THE PURSUIT OF LOVE?

❧

I have learned so much from relationships. The last long-term relationship I had lasted four and a half years.

Throughout the relationship, I noticed several things happening. He was always the one who chose where we went and what we did. The few times I chose the location for our dates, he had "attitude."

He was very insecure, and if I didn't worship the ground he walked on, he would stomp out of the house, slamming the door behind him.

He threw three temper tantrums in public, probably more.

He had road rage. He was good about driving but I was uncomfortable riding with him. I confronted him about this, but he refused to change.

I started walking on eggshells. Trying not to get him upset. I stopped confronting him. I gave up all the things I wanted to go to. I did this to please him, yet he remained temperamental and unhappy.

I felt torn inside. He was good to me in so many ways, but there was something wrong. I could feel it. Something was changing, and I didn't like the change. I was losing myself, becoming a shadow of him and dimming the limelight I had once been.

One of my girlfriends put it so well when she said, "When I first met you, you were vibrant and alive. He is stealing you little by little. You are not the same person you were when we met."

I could tell she missed me. I missed myself more.

During those years, I gave up my writing. I tried to write, but every time I asked to have a weekend at home alone, he would accuse me of cheating on him. So, I stopped asking for solitary time.

I finally confronted him about the future of our relationship. I found out he wanted me to sell my house. That was the only thing I had left, which I loved, that was mine. I ended the relationship.

I began trying to find myself. I rediscovered writing. I found it an avenue for self-discovery. It is a breathtaking, beautiful path back to me, and I am finding myself to be someone who is worthy of true love.

Writing is my calling from God and my destiny. I hope in the midst of this journey I may find a man who is worthy of my love.

PROVERBS *29:22 An angry person starts fights; a hot-tempered person commits all kinds of sin. (NLT)*

Do your relationships nurture the things which breathe life into you? List the benefits of your current relationship.

ARE you compromising your destiny to fulfill someone else's desires? If so, why?

MISTRESS-WHICH BASE IS SHE PLAYING?

❧

I have had several friends over the years who have had affairs with married men. I tried to understand why they had made that choice. They were young. They should have been looking for a husband they could start a family with. What made them want someone unavailable?

In one case, the man was higher up in the company than my girlfriend was. Did the affair help her career?

Another one got involved with a coworker. He ended up leaving his family for her and living off her income after he got fired.

Another one was a friend of a friend. The mistress was a flight attendant, the man a pilot. The affair lasted a very long time. By the time I met her, she was old, unattractive, and desperate. The pilot had used up her cute years, and she had freely given him that right.

A married man approached me when I was newly divorced. I was a nurse and working in a nursing home. The doctor who was the medical director started taking a fancy to me. He rubbed up against me in a patient's room. It was a very uncomfortable situation to be in.

He had a reputation for having several girlfriends besides a wife. I tried to avoid him. One day when I was charting, he sat down next to me, and he started becoming "handsy." He said, "If this is bothering you, let me know."

I looked at him and said, "You have a wife and a girlfriend. You aren't ever going to have me because I don't play second or third base. I play first base or nothing at all."

He removed his hand, and we remained professionals, which is all we should have been to start with.

If you are a mistress to a married man, I hope you realize there is more cheating going on than you realize. You are also cheating yourself.

Proverbs 6:32 The one who commits adultery lacks sense; whoever does so destroys himself. (NIRV)

ARE you in a relationship with a married man?

CAN you identify steps to break free of this?

AN INTERNET DATING SCAM

everal years ago, a scammer approached me on an internet dating site. The guy had his address listed in a nearby suburb and when he contacted me; I replied. I wasn't too interested–his occupation was landscaper. When he started messaging me, he transformed from a landscaper nearby to an oil executive in Nigeria. My hopes went up. That should have been the first warning sign.

He sent me a picture. He was nice looking, not breathtaking, but better than average.

He had a son; I believe the son was staying in Holland. He had lost his wife in a tragic car accident. Second warning sign.

He tapped into my nurturing instinct, and I was hooked. His instant messages became the highlight of my day. He seemed to have ESP when I was on the computer. No wonder the creep's job was to scam. No need to walk away from a computer when you have that kind of job.

I never talked to him on the phone. Thank God.

I really thought that a future would be possible with this man. (I know, sometimes I can be beyond naïve.)

Then his story started getting weird.

He said he had taken a day off to go shopping and had bought an antique bronze skull in the village. (Who the heck bronzes a skull?!!) Then he said he didn't have money to get the skull back to the states (btw oil executives always have money) and he wanted to give it to me.

Gosh, I thought about all the things I wanted to decorate my house with, and the last thing was an antique bronze skull! (Red flags were waving sky high).

He further said that I needed to be an interloper in a business transaction between someone who would pick something up from my mailbox and send it to Nigeria. By the way, he didn't trust this person who was supposed to be coming to my mailbox, which was right in front of my house.

WHAT?!!!

By this time, there were many problems I had with this potential suitor.

Number 1 He wanted to involve me in an international money transaction and there was NO WAY I WAS GOING TO DO THAT! (I could get myself thrown into jail for that kind of stupid.) I watch my money like a hawk, and if I don't know where or what it is financing; it stays in my pocket! This man could be linked to terrorists, a drug cartel, or could be a kid in a Nigerian sweat factory who preys on American women to scam them.

Number 2 I do not enable people in their weaknesses. If this was really a business transaction, then he needed to pay for it.

Number 3 Who in their right mind would buy an antique bronze head and pay $1,500 for it?

Number 4 I am a single mother with three amazing children. Let me get this right... He wanted me to give him my address to give to someone he didn't trust?!! The answer is NOT IN MY LIFETIME!

I ended the scam by saying, "Sounds like quite the pickle you have gotten into, but this is your pickle to deal with, not mine."

No further instant messages came.

Proverbs 26:28 A lying tongue hates its victims, and flattering words cause ruin. (NLT)

The reason I got on the internet dating site was to find love. The verse in Proverbs is so powerful. If someone lies to you, they do not love you; they hate you.

To read more information about internet dating scams please click on the following link.https://www.consumer.ftc.gov/articles/what-you-need-know-about-romance-scams

Do you justify dishonesty for the sake of "love?"

Do you lie to others in the disguise of "loving them?"

Do you realize that when you lie to someone, you are not loving them but hating them?

Are you in a relationship with someone who is dishonest?

THE BEAUTY OF A BROKEN HEART

❧

Suffering a broken heart is anguish, but it is not without benefit. A heart which has not been hurt may still beat but not nearly as strong and as vibrant as a heart which, torn to shreds, struggles to survive. Once the broken heart beats again, it is encased with thick scars from the battle.

Both are beautiful hearts, but the one with scars may not be so enthralled with its own beauty. This heart looks outward to see the crevices in another's heart, rushing in to stop the bleeding with love and encouragement.

The obsession with its own beauty is long past gone because of the scars betrayal has left. Through healing the broken heart realizes one of the greatest gifts you can get is to give, not receive, love. For if it is all about receiving, then the pain may return if you don't receive. If it is instead about giving love, then the power lies within the giving.

That is the beauty of a broken heart.

Psalms 34:18 The lord is near to the brokenhearted and saves the crushed in spirit. (CSB)

. . .

GRACIE LYNNE

HAS YOUR HEART BEEN BROKEN?

IF SO, do you seek to show love to others after healing your heart?

MISERY LOVES COMPANY

When you are a single parent or are going through a divorce, it is wise to vet the company you keep.

I had someone close to me that had not come to a point of forgiveness in their own life. Because of this failure, their heart was bound with bitterness. They made me believe I needed to tell them everything after my divorce: what I was doing, who I was dating, and what my ex-husband had done to hurt me recently.

They wanted their monster fed. In feeding their bitterness, I sunk deeper into the black chasm of my own despair. This did nothing to help me.

It just made me feel more like a victim. I hate being a victim.

A phone call to someone, who is now a good friend, helped me out of my depression.

It was a phone call about my finances, which have been meager since my marriage to my ex, some years ago. I was discussing a refinance on my house with this stranger, and I broke down in tears.

He did not fall for my victim's act. He told me I was not a victim.

What? How did he know? I thought I had that role down pat. I surely had heard enough stories of victimhood from the person who had been bound in bitterness.

He told me I needed to be strong and then helped me with my re-finance. He finished the call by praying over me.

Whenever I think of him, I think of him with gratefulness, not anger or indignation. He helped me stand on my own two feet, strong and independent, encouraging me not to get lost in my pain.

I have learned some people feed off the pain of others to make themselves feel better.

Others use pain to feed the monster of bitterness within their own heart. They may not even see the disease within their own soul, but if you are wise, you will see it and run from it.

It is one thing to offer comfort and solutions to a person who is fighting a battle. It is a far different thing to make them feel there is no way to win their battle because you have not won yours.

Proverbs 13:20 "Walk with the wise and become wise, associate with fools, and get in trouble." (NLT)

WHO ARE the people you turn to for comfort?

Do they encourage you to fight the battle with courage, or do you feel more defeated after confiding in them?

HOW OFTEN DO you turn to God and ask for the Holy Spirit to comfort you and give you guidance?

THE ADDICTION OF INTERNET DATING

❦

I am an addict; I admit it. I am an internet dating addict. Every day, at least once or twice a day, I check my inbox daily to find Mr. Wonderful.

He is not there.

Have I dated? You bet I have.

Did I have fun on those dates? For the most part, yes.

Did I meet some worthy, handsome and successful gentlemen? Yep, I met some great guys and had some wonderful dates.

So why did I take down my profiles on both dating sites recently?

It was too easy to discard men and maybe myself. If it didn't work out with one man, there would always be another one waiting.

Plus, there was the tension, the conflict within my soul, of wanting to be a Christian, yet walking into the trap of temptation. Most people subscribe to dating sites for one reason. That reason is sex.

Today I had lunch with a good Christian man who I had met on OK Cupid. He asked me how I handled the world's view of premarital sex when I was a Christian.

I confessed I hadn't had a history of handling it very well. I tried not to succumb to temptation but had, at times, compromised my Christian values. According to men I have dated, the women on

Christian Mingle are as sex starved as women on other sites. The men are no better; they date to satisfy their flesh.

They have the same disease as I have. The disease is hypocrisy. I have become sickened at my hypocrisy regarding premarital sex.

I have confessed my sin, but have I repented? It is my understanding that repentance is turning away from sin and walking the other way. I am now at the point of repentance, pleading with God for forgiveness.

Why now?

I have learned the futility of premarital sex. Sex without marriage cheapens love and opens the door for Satan to grasp your heart. Sex becomes the primary focus of the relationship and genuine love is lost in the pursuit of sex.

I had a boyfriend who loved me for my beauty and treated me like a sex object. He called me the "love of his life."

We argued constantly. Every time I needed him to support me, he would abandon me. Although he is no longer my boyfriend, I learned so much from that relationship.

I learned that if a man loves your body without the commitment of marriage, he may not see your true beauty.

Your body is temporal, your soul is eternal. If you have premarital sex, you may sacrifice eternal love for temporal pleasure. Is it really worth it?

1 Corinthians 6:18-20 - Flee fornication. *Every sin that a man doeth is without the body; but he that committeth* fornication *sinneth against his own body. (KJV)*

WHAT IS your opinion on premarital sex?

DO your opinions and behavior line up with God's word?

THE PROMISE OF SIN

I had a very busy day today. One highlight of my day was having brunch with my friend David Roberts.

Have you ever talked with someone, and you had to stop several times during the conversation because the other person was just tossing out wisdom? Well, that is how my brunch went with David Roberts.

When someone is speaking wisdom, I grab whatever is available and try to catch a quote. I write the quote down on napkins, table-cloths, (paper of course) or, in this case, a sales receipt.

David gave me a winning quote today and I want to share it with you. Drum roll, please...

The quote is:

"THE PROMISE OF SIN IS TO SERVE AND TO PLEASE WHEN IT'S TRUE DESIRE IS TO DOMINATE AND DESTROY."

That is just about the smartest thing that I have ever heard.

IF YOU ARE INVOLVED in a relationship based on lust and not love, are you aware of the cost?

. . .

JOHN 8:31-32 Jesus said to the people who believed in him. "You are truly my disciples if you remain faithful to my teachings. (32) And you will know the truth, and the truth will set you free." (NSRV)

Do you think lust is essential to a lifetime of love? I am referring to lust here, not physical attraction. I think attraction is necessary for a relationship. Explain the difference between lust and love.

WHO HAS THE FINAL VOTE?

I met a guy some time ago who gave me an interesting proposition. We hadn't even had a drink before he presented a dilemma.

He said he had met this woman a while before he asked me out. She had come over to his house and was planning to go to Vegas. She was intent upon meeting up with a producer in Vegas, which apparently, she did. While at his house, she decided she wanted his input on her wardrobe for the Vegas trip. So, she went out to her car, retrieved her suitcase, did a striptease, and then modeled her different outfits that she intended to wear while in Vegas.

He claims he didn't have sex with her. My mouth dropped open in disbelief on that one.

This guy told me this story and believe it or not, it actually intrigued me enough not to spit my drink out all over him.

Then he says that this woman gets to vote on who he marries. At that point, I had to stop drinking, otherwise I was going to vomit my drink all over his chest.

He asked if I had any problem with that.

"Yeah, I do. First, I am not interested in marriage, at least not on the first date."

"Second, I don't dig another woman having more of a say so in my relationships than I do."

"Third, I am a Christian, and God, not some "has been" stripper, gets the vote on who I marry."

He didn't get a second date.

Job 5:8-9"As for me, I would seek God, and to God would I commit my cause, who does great things and unsearchable, marvelous things without number." (KJV)

WHO GETS the final vote on your potential spouse?

HOW WOULD you have responded to this dilemma?

IS GOD MY MATCHMAKER?

I have had little luck in the dating department lately. Some of that is because of my quitting the internet dating sites, but I kind of think God has his hand in it too.

A few weeks ago, I went to a social gathering that was for singles, and it was at a nearby club. I had fun, and one certain guy started hitting on me. I liked him, but not enough to date him.

He asked me out the next weekend. He asked me to meet him at a marvelous place, so I figured I would go just as a friend. The whole time I was driving into town, I was praying. When I got there, I looked around for him and couldn't find him. So, I drove back home.

He texted me about two hours later and told me he had fallen asleep. I told him to get lost. I realized that this was my answer to prayer. God put the sleep on him. Lol

Then tonight I was going to give a guy one last chance to grab my heart. This guy has been a flake from the start, but I keep giving him chances.

Well, tonight he flaked out again and said his water heater started leaking. I imagine that could happen, but for a man who is a construction manager for a commercial real estate company like this man is, I think he should have things like that under control.

I won't be responding to any more text messages or phone calls from him because I blocked his number.

I am thankful God is protecting me by being my matchmaker. He knows the hearts of men better than I do, and He also knows I am not a pushover.

If a guy or girl keeps brushing you off, don't take it personally. They are not worth a second thought. As it says in the Bible shake the dust off your feet.

Matthew 10:14 Any city or home that doesn't welcome you—shake off the dust of that place from your feet as you leave.

Proverbs 19:21 Many are the plans in the mind of a man, but it is the purpose of the LORD that will stand. (ESV)

WHO IS your matchmaker in the dating game?

DO you commit your dates to God?

A DIFFERENT GIRLFRIEND

I am a different kind of girlfriend. Whenever I go on dates, I analyze the person I meet and try to figure out exactly what God needs me to do in the relationship.

One thing He doesn't need me to do is to take my clothes off.

The other thing I refuse to do is demean or devalue the last girlfriend or wife the man is trying to get over.

I try not to open up the door to being a psychoanalyst, but sometimes these men need counseling so badly I want to give them a referral.

I also do not pick up the tab. I expect the man that I marry to be in a position where he can pay the bills and whatever I make will be the added blessing. To pay the tab on a date is to put on a front that I am not willing to continue in marriage.

This is different if we have established boundaries of friendship before the date. In that case, I always pay my own tab.

Lately I have dated two men who are still in love with their former wives. They are both attracted to me, but I am standing true to God's principles for dating, and I have resisted any physical involvement.

Although one of them is going through the process of divorce and the other one is fresh out of a divorce, I feel that crossing the line into intimacy would be wrong. It would mess with their heart when their heart had not healed yet.

This morning I had to keep standing my ground with the latest man. He finally backed down. I will continue to see him, because, for a change, he builds me up and is very encouraging to me. I am usually the one who is constantly doing that, and it is nice to have someone return the favor.

Recently, a man told me if I wanted to wait until marriage for sex, I would not get many dates. That hasn't been the case. I still date frequently, but I do so with Jesus' sacrifice and God's mandates first and foremost in my mind. If I want to attract the man that God has for me, then why would I choose to walk down Satan's path to get him?

1 Corinthians 6:13 You say, "Food for the stomach and the stomach for food, and God will destroy them both." The body, however, is not meant for sexual immorality but for the Lord, and the Lord for the body. (NIV)

WHAT MAKES you a unique person to date?

Do you hold on to your values when dating or do you compromise?

WHAT DO you think your body was created for?

WHO CAN HEAL A BROKEN HEART?

There are some who think therapy can heal a broken heart. The unwrapping of your life to reveal the wounds of childhood may help some people. However, I have always wondered how looking through the broken window of your past can transform your future.

Many think that if they just find the right partner, all will be better again. Partners can add to life, but they can also make life more challenging.

Success is a great band aid for a broken heart, but I know some successful people who were cruel to the people who helped them achieve their success. Cruelty can result from a heart not properly healed.

Wisdom is different than psychology. The times I have searched God for wisdom are the times I have felt the power of healing in my heart. The counsel of the Holy Spirit has exposed deep-seated motivations for behaviors I have, which harm me and others.

It is this counsel which I consider worthy to heal my heart. Nothing else has come close to the counsel of the Holy Spirit.

Psalms 147:3 He heals the brokenhearted and binds up their wounds. (ESV)

John 14:25-27 "I'm telling you these things while I'm still living with you. The Friend, the Holy Spirit whom the Father will send at my request, will make everything plain to you. He will remind you of all the things I have told you. I'm leaving you well and whole. That's my parting gift to you. Peace. I don't leave you the way you're used to being left—feeling abandoned, bereft. So don't be upset. Don't be distraught. (The Message)

WHO CAN HEAL your broken heart?

HAVE you submitted your tears and fractured emotions to God?

HAVE you asked God to reveal His plan and His love for you in the midst of a broken heart?

A CHAPERONE FOR A DATE?

I have gotten into a habit lately when I go on dates. I invite God on the date. It is amazing at how wonderful my dates have been since I extended this invitation.

It is also uncanny that I have had no chemistry with any of the men whom I have dated since God has been my chaperone. I used to have chemistry with everything *and* a brick wall.

I rarely date separated men, but a couple of weeks ago I met one for drinks and an appetizer at a nearby restaurant. As is usually the case with separated men, the conversation revolved around his wife. She had recently left him after twenty-five years of marriage. I could tell that he still loved her. He said she had made him happy for twenty-five years.

She, on the other hand, had gone to California to meet another man. I figured it was someone she met on the internet.

We had a pleasant time and parted. He called me last week. I wasn't able to answer the call. I called him back today. Once again, the conversation was about his wife. I am so glad that I am past the stage in life where I think it needs to be all about me on dates.

I rarely preach, but this dear man got himself one doozy of a sermon today.

I found out his wife had gone to California to hook up with a man who had previously abused her. My friend had promised to protect his wife from this abusive man when he married her. Now she leaves him for the abuser? Something is very messed up with that situation.

I told him he needed to do everything he could to win her back because he still loved her. I would be nothing other than a friend to him because this involved a covenant with God, which I believe could be reconciled. I gave him the biggest pep talk I have ever given any man to push him into another woman's arms. I think that is why God nudged me to call him today. Everyone else was encouraging him to let her go.

This man has not gone crazy trying to find another woman to sleep with. He has instead prayed unceasingly, read the Bible, and has sought godly counsel. He is a worthy man of God.

It is amazing at how a date can develop into a testimony when God is invited.

JOHN 14:16-17 *And I will ask the Father, and he will give you another Helper, to be with you forever, even the Spirit of truth, whom the world cannot receive, because it neither sees him nor knows him. You know him, for he dwells with you and will be in you. (NKJV)*

Do you use your dates to glorify God?

Do you find your Christian journey better when dating or worse?

FEAR

I had an emotional roller coaster of a day yesterday. Fear was knocking at my front door. I was worried about my financial future.

Unfortunately, I revealed my fear to an acquaintance who didn't think my fear was warranted. The conversation with this man via text messages was confusing to me. He couldn't understand my fear, and in the process of our conversation, my fear deepened.

I was trying to understand exactly why God had even allowed this man to contact me when I got a phone call. It was from a woman that I had met at a networking event. We were supposed to have coffee in the afternoon and talk about the different businesses we were involved in.

She had been a single mother for ten years. *She* understood my fear. She sent me a link to an encouraging sermon via text message and prayed over me.

Even though I cancelled the coffee date in the afternoon because I thought it would be a waste of time for her, she still showed me the love of Christ. She had walked the path I have walked as a single mother. She *knew* my fear.

But does God know my fear? When Jesus came down to earth, He came as a man. He had the Spirit of God within Him, but yet, He was human.

He was tempted just as we are, maybe more so; I have yet to go without food for forty days and then have the devil offer me a loaf of bread.

The destination of Christ was crucifixion, but with every step to the cross, He was human. He overcame the world, but He did not overcome it without being a part of it. He understands us, just as my friend understood me yesterday.

The love of God astounds me. He could have sent His son down to earth as a King. That is what the Jews were looking for. They wanted a king to deliver them, but if Christ had been a King, would He be able to understand *us*? A King would not have understood the fear I felt yesterday.

I know Christ understood because He was human. He doesn't sit in his high heaven looking down with condemnation on me for my sins. He looks at me through the brilliant prism of understanding and compassion. Through understanding comes forgiveness, which is the consummate reason God became man through His son, Jesus Christ.

Hebrews 2:17–18 Therefore, he had to be made like his brothers in every respect, so that he might become a merciful and faithful high priest in the service of God, to make propitiation for the sins of the people. For because he himself has suffered when tempted, he is able to help those who are being tempted. (ESV)

Do you feel as if Jesus understands your weaknesses?

Do you have friends who have walked your path who can empathize with you?

WHEN GOD TAKES CONTROL

I said a brief prayer this morning and asked God to be a part of my day. I had to get up early because I had an appointment at the dealership for a recall notice.

I was late—my normal—this time worse than usual. I pulled into the dealership 30 minutes after the time I had said I would arrive. When I got there, they said they may have to order the part, and I may need to come back another day to get the work done.

I replied with a smile, "How long do you think it will take you to figure this out?"

The man said he would get me the info ASAP. Then he directed me to the customer lounge.

I walked in with half a cup of coffee. I glanced over and saw a portly old man who immediately introduced himself to me and said they had no coffee in the lounge. He stated there was coffee in the other lounge, though. He also told me he had been married for 52 years and would be happy to watch my purse while I walked over to get some coffee.

Not that I didn't trust him, but my purse has handles and I can carry my cup and my purse with no problem. So, the purse came with me. I did let him babysit my Kindle and a book I was reading. My Kindle is my most cherished gift from my children, so that was a big thing.

After I put my reading items down on a chair, I glanced at him quickly and asked him if he would like a cup of coffee.

He lit up and said, "Yes!" Then proceeded to profusely thank me. I made the check for cream and sugar. He drank coffee with no additives, just like me. I set out to go fetch the coffee. I warmed up my coffee and got a cup for him, then made my way back to the customer lounge where he sat.

As soon as I had given him his coffee, the man from the dealership said they did not have my part in, and I would have to come back in a couple of days.

I said, "Well, I guess I drove here just to get you your cup of coffee." A smile crossed my face. I didn't accomplish what I set out to do this morning, but I accomplished so much more. I could give a man a cup of coffee and brighten his day.

I drove home with a smile splitting my cheeks. I love it when God takes control and sends me out as a messenger of His love. It took less than an hour, but it made my whole day.

Matthew 10:42 "And whoever, because he is a disciple, gives one of these little ones even a cup of cold water (or coffee) to drink, I tell you the truth, he will by no means lose his reward." (Mounce)

Do you submit your day to God while in the throes of waking up?

Is it important to you to do something for others as well as yourself every day?

. . .

Do you experience joy when you put your agenda aside and embrace the agenda of God?

CHOOSING THE RIGHT ONE

❧

*T*here are many people in the world today who are unhappily married. I was talking with a new friend about this today, and I told him I thought I knew the reason.

When you date someone and there is chemistry, it is very easy to cross the line into sex. Bravo to those who have resisted.

Once you cross that line, you justify the relationship according to a standard other than God's. You become complacent about the things you were originally bothered by, especially if the sex is good.

A quote by Thomas Cranmer puts this dilemma in perfect words.

"What the heart loves, the will chooses and the mind justifies."

In James 4, it says we become double minded when we walk in sin. We know better, but we succumb to fleshly lusts and then we get distracted from the purpose and destiny God has created us for. We cannot see the other person clearly when we do this because sin blinds, and there is no better blinder than lust.

I would encourage those of you who are single Christians to seek God first and only Him. In James 4, it says to flee from the devil. If you cannot resist temptation, may I suggest you always meet in a public place and during the daylight hours?

If it is His will for you to marry again, He will make it happen the right way. It is difficult, if not impossible, to get to heaven by walking the path of Satan. You can't get to paradise by walking through hell.

James 4:8 Draw near to God, and He will draw near to you. Cleanse your hands, you sinners, and purify your hearts, you double-minded!(ESV)

WHAT BOUNDARIES DO you set for dates?

HOW ARE you honoring God in your current relationships?

THE "WOW" MAN

❦

I have met someone new. This morning we met for coffee, and I saw a side of him I hadn't seen before.

We initially met through a social group and sat next to each other until another guy bulldozed his way in between us. Then he started talking to some other women, and I talked to the bulldozer guy.

I left early, and he asked me why. I don't remember why, but I always have a list of a thousand things to do, so that was probably why.

We exchanged phone numbers, and I told him I thought he would be a good fit for my MLM business. Our first date was mostly about business, but we shared a bit of personal drama as well.

The next date was when we really clicked. The conversation was amazing. He actually gets me! He likes the way I think! I didn't think anyone would ever get me! Lol.

Plus, it impressed him that I have chosen to be celibate because of my honor of God. He says he is attracted to my heart, not my body.

This morning, I swear someone else was inside of him. He tried to make me jealous, saying he had found the other two women he had talked with at the social event very interesting. They had also expressed interest in him. He is a successful doctor and a very sweet man, so I did not find that surprising.

He also indicated he would be busy on Valentine's day with a homeless ministry he was involved in.

Then he kept trying to kiss me. I kept pushing him away.

When I came home, I regurgitated the date. I wasn't angry with him, but contemplated just how I was going to handle this. I wanted to kick him to the curb.

I told God if He wanted me to continue seeing this man, He was going to have to handle this.

I thought about it some more and then had an "Aha" moment. I am getting those a lot more since I have been pursuing *God*. If he was going to be busy on the 14th of February, I could be too. I sent him the following text.

"The more I think of it, the more I am impressed you are doing the homeless ministry on Valentine's day. That gives me the freedom to accept one of the many invitations I have already received. You are SOOO CONSIDERATE!"

(DISCLAIMER–I have received no invitations yet but my goodness, it is only January 11th- I mean REALLY!)

Two minutes later a text came back "Can you talk?"

I refused, saying I was busy, and I was busy.

Two minutes after that he texted, "I have not agreed to work on Valentine's day. I was just invited." I may have heard him wrong, so I will give him that one.

An hour later, I checked my messages, and he said he wanted to talk to me about his daughter. He got me there. I called him.

The first thing I heard from him was, "I'm sorry."

"What?" I asked in surprise, moving to my bed because I thought I might faint.

He said it again.

This has got to be a record! I have only known this man a little over a week, and he is humble enough to say he is sorry not once but twice?!!

"You are sorry for what?" I asked.

"For manipulating you. That is what I used to do, and I am trying to change that."

I have one word for this man. "WOW!"

I could not be more impressed with him at this point. He tried to introduce fear into our relationship through the door of jealousy, and I called him on it. Instead of running, fighting me or degrading me, he took ownership for the wrong he did, and said he was trying to change his behavior.

This opened up the door to me, acknowledging the games I play and some manipulation I do. His humility melted my heart this afternoon and through his humility, I became humble as well.

Just a thought for those of us who think that fighting or fear is the way to win someone's heart. I think this man could teach us all a lesson.

The other lesson that could be gleaned from this story is that if you have a problem with another person, take it to God first. He is the one who is in the business of transforming hearts, and somehow, when we try doing that, we usually break them.

Unfortunately, this man did not change his ways long-term. He continued to talk about other women every time we met. I tenderly ended any hopes of a committed relationship but consider him a friend.

James 5:16 Confess your faults one to another, and pray one for another, that ye may be healed. The effectual fervent prayer of a righteous man availeth much. (KJV)

WHAT BEHAVIORS DO you do which could be considered manipulation?

ARE you dating someone who is humble enough to take ownership of their manipulation and ask for forgiveness?

. . .

IF THE MANIPULATION CONTINUES, are you confident enough to end the relationship?

BUT HE SINNED!

*have had quite a wonderful dating experience since I have been single. I have also had the unfortunate experience of dating more than a few men who have not rendered a second date.

The latest man I met has caused me to reflect in a deeper way how I choose conversational topics. Usually, the conversation gets steered to the reasons they are single. I have heard more about ex-wives than sports teams, and if they don't have ex-wives; it is the ex-girlfriends I have heard about.

I don't mind them talking about their past loves, but it is no foundation upon which to build a relationship.

My recent man of interest talked to me a bit about his marriage and admitted he had sinned in the relationship. Of course, not surprisingly, he blamed the ex-wife. We all play the blame game, starting with Adam and Eve. I have done so too.

I have prayed and contemplated whether I want to dig deeper with this man. I am someone who can analyze a person down to their most microscopic cell. I definitely overthink most things.

As I prayed about this relationship, I realized it would do nothing for this man to confess his sin to me. I am not his savior. I do not know his heart. Only God does. It is not for me to forgive him. It is for God and his ex-wife.

It is my duty to encourage him and edify him in the good qualities I see in him, and those are very many; much more than I have seen in most men.

It is also my privilege to intercede for him in prayer, hoping that he will draw close to God and seek Him, not me, for forgiveness and healing of the heart.

I already see God opening places in his heart, which were locked for many years. It is not my place to grab the key from God and unlock his heart. For if I do, I risk those doors to his heart being locked forever.

If I choose to play God, I am choosing the wrong role to play, for my blood saves no one from their sin.

Galatians 6:1 Dear brothers and sisters, if another believer is overcome by some sin, you who are godly should gently and humbly help that person back onto the right path. And be careful not to fall into the same temptation yourself. (NLT)

HOW DO you respond to someone else confessing sin to you?

Do you try to fix people, or do you pray for God to fix them?

HOW TO MAKE GOD CRY

$\mathcal{I}$n Ephesians 4:30-32, the Bible says that we can grieve the Holy Spirit. We actually can make God cry.

I have just suffered through three of the most horrific years of my life, and I have noticed when another attack was happening many times, it would be raining. I used to think God was crying with me as my heart was breaking. I don't doubt He felt my pain, and had compassion on me, maybe even to the point of making it rain, but now I see things differently.

I may have caused Him to cry during those times. When I screamed out at Him, "Where are you, God, and why are you not doing *anything* to stop this evil?!" My heart was filled with indignation and pain, far from the land of forgiveness.

In *Ephesians 4:30*, it says, "*And do not grieve the Holy Spirit of God, with whom you were sealed for the day of redemption.*"

How on earth could I grieve God?

"*By holding bitterness, rage and anger, brawling, and slander along with every form of malice in my heart.*" (*Ephesians 4:31*) These emotions are insurmountable obstacles to God's love and forgiveness.

It does not matter what someone else has done to me on my judgment day. All that matters is how I treat other people and the response

I have to evil. Is it more important to hold evil in my heart or to *block evil* so nothing stops the love of God from entering in and flowing out to others?

So how do I stop evil? By being kind and compassionate, forgiving others, just as in Christ, God forgave me. To do this to those who seek to harm me is to walk away from Satan and walk back into the loving embrace of God.

Ephesians 4:30-32 30 And do not grieve the Holy Spirit of God, by whom you were sealed for the day of redemption. 31 Let all bitterness and wrath and anger and clamor and slander be put away from you, along with all malice. 32 Be kind to one another, tenderhearted, forgiving one another, as God in Christ forgave you. (ESV)

How do you respond to unfair accusations?

How do you respond to someone attacking you and taking advantage of you?

Are you open to forgiving those who have done you wrong?

THE RULE OF THREE

*D*o you feel as if you are compromising your values and standards in order to secure "love" in a relationship?

Why do we continue to put our hearts on the line when, even in a baseball game, a person is out on strike three?

May I suggest a rule for relationships? If someone disrespects your boundaries, only let it happen three times. The first time confront the individual and tell him/her that their actions, attitude, or words are unacceptable.

The second time remind them in a very firm tone of voice this is unacceptable and will not nurture any feelings of love.

The third time, walk away and don't look back.

I have wasted so much of my life giving people multiple breaks and second chances in relationships.

If a person lies to you once and you catch them at it, then put your antennas up.

If they lie to you again, it is time to make your exit plan.

Three times and they are out of your life, and they were probably lying all along, so don't shed a tear.

This rule can apply to many things. Road rage, profanity, temper tantrums, acting the fool around someone else when they should focus on you, disrespecting your boundaries, and trashing your possessions.

If you think this isn't Christian, then reflect on Jesus and the following verses in Luke. He didn't give this crowd a second chance. He passed right through them. Continuing in a relationship which is full of deceit and toxicity is not beneficial to God's plan for your life.

Luke 4:28-30 "When they heard this, everyone in the synagogue was enraged. They got up, drove him out of town, and brought him to the edge of the hill that their town was built on, intending to hurl him over the cliff. But he passed right through the crowd and went on his way." (CSB)

HOW MANY CHANCES do you give a person?

DO you think giving someone three chances is too many? I would agree in the instance of abuse.

WHAT THINGS DO you consider unacceptable in a relationship?

EVE

I was reading Genesis, reflecting on the meaning of Eve. The name, Eve, means to breathe life, but I believe it is also the root word of evening. I continued to let my mind wander, thinking of the significance of this name.

As women, we should breathe life into relationships. We should make the relationship vibrant with beauty. We should also seek peace and comfort for our loved one, bringing calm just as an *evening* sunset does.

God formed Eve out of the rib of Adam. Which may be symbolic of her role. There is a quote from Augustine of Hippo which puts this so beautifully...

"A woman came from a man's rib, not from the legs to be humiliated, not from the head to excel. But from the side, to be side by side with him, to be equal with him. From under the arm, to be protected and from the heart to be loved."

GENESIS 3:20 Adam[a] named his wife Eve,[b] because she would become the mother of all the living. (NIV

Do you find you are walking side by side with those you date or want to date? Or do you feel inferior or superior to them?

Are you breathing life into your dating relationship?

LESSONS OF LOVE

$\mathcal{I}$ have learned so many lessons of love during my years of dating.

I have learned it doesn't matter what kind of car the man drives. If he is rude, he will not notice you are a gem.

I have learned if I date a gentleman, he will still be a gentleman even if I decide the relationship is not what I want long term.

I have learned if you tolerate a man acting like a fool and exploding with anger at frequent intervals, they will continue to act like a two-year-old. As a former pastor said, "You have what you tolerate in life."

I have learned my happiness is important. If a man is asking me to abandon my dreams to follow his, then he wants me to sacrifice my joy so that he can be in control.

I have learned if a man is addicted to alcohol or cigarettes, that toxicity seeps out of his pores and into my life in more ways than I can count.

I have learned love is just a word and a very meaningless word if not followed by actions and attitude.

I have learned I have an obligation to pursue my own happiness, whether in or out of a relationship. My happiness is *my* responsibility and *not* dependent on anyone else.

I have learned to have sex on the first date is animal-like behavior. If you have sex without knowing someone you put your heart and your body in a precarious state.

I have learned when you allow sin into a relationship, God will still love you, but he will not stop the consequences of the sin.

I have learned God understands women and most of the commandments regarding sex were written to protect the woman. The woman often desires love, while a man finds satisfaction in the physical relationship.

I have learned to go on a date without inviting the spirit of God is just not fun and I like to have fun.

I have learned although many men are interested in me, not one would sacrifice His only son to die for all the wickedness I have done, and that, my dear, is true love.

John 3:16

16 For God so loved the world that he gave his one and only Son, that whoever believes in him shall not perish but have eternal life.

WHAT LESSONS HAVE you learned from dating?

HAVE these lessons enhanced your relationship with God or diminished it?

EVICTION NOTICE

What would you do if you had a tenant in an exquisite mansion that tore the home apart? What if they allowed their animals to defecate on the white carpet? The house was so messy that to find a path to walk through the house was more difficult than finding Waldo. Although the initial rental agreement stated that they would be responsible for landscaping, they refused to mow the lawn. Last time you checked, they piled the dishes up in the sink and cockroaches were on the kitchen counter.

It wouldn't take me long to give an eviction notice.

Now I want you to use your imagination and pretend your mind is the mansion.

What kind of thoughts, memories, and emotions do you rent space to?

Do you focus on all the hurtful memories?

Do you ruminate about what that narcissist said?

Do you replay the act of betrayal which stabbed your heart with pain?

It is a human fallacy to believe time spent dwelling on negative things will change them into positive.

In Philippians 4:8 Paul says, "Finally, brethren, whatever things are true, whatever things are noble, whatever things are just, whatever things are pure, whatever things are lovely, whatever things are of good report, if there is any virtue and if there is anything praiseworthy-meditate on these things."

It appears as if we are not to ruminate about the evil that has been done to us. If we choose to focus on the evil; we open the door to Satan's plans for our life. So next time a terrible memory seeps in through your door, give it an eviction notice and open the door to what is good instead.

Next time you remember something a person did to you that hurt you try to remember a time when they showed love to you instead.

Philippians 4:8 "Finally, brethren, whatever things are true, whatever things are noble, whatever things are just, whatever things are pure, whatever things are lovely, whatever things are of good report, if there is any virtue and if there is anything praiseworthy-meditate on these things." (NKJV)

Do you focus on the good or bad that has happened to you?

Do you need to evict some thoughts from your mind?

FORGIVENESS

When someone offends you, do you forgive them? What if they keep offending you, saying ugly and negative things about you?

What if they have betrayed you? If they have lied to you, do you trust them ever again?

It depends on how you view forgiveness.

If you view it as a gift to them, you may want to hold on to it. They really don't deserve a gift. If you view forgiveness instead as a gift to yourself, you may be more apt to give it freely.

Think about it. When someone is nasty, and you keep that in your heart, how do you feel? When someone is rude, and you are rude back, doesn't that make you more like them?

I read a book last week that gave a very interesting interpretation to forgiveness.

The book was "Estranged" by Jessica Berger Gross. It was about a life of a child who had been physically abused by her father.

In this book, the main character sought the counsel of a female rabbi to seek the meaning of forgiveness.

The rabbi's response was: "The Hebrew word *teshuvah* usually gets translated as 'forgiveness,' but the true meaning is a 'return to your finest self.'"

"Forgiveness," she continued, "is a process we go through with someone else. It's not instantaneous. It can take years to say I'm sorry, and years to forgive. And sometimes it doesn't happen."

Forgiveness is returning to your finer self–before the betrayal, lies, abuse and negativity harmed you.

The people who continually do harm to others will remain just that-harmful and nasty. If we hold on to our bitterness, we will soon become like them.

Colossians 3:13 bearing with one another and, if one has a complaint against another, forgiving each other; as the Lord has forgiven you, so you also must forgive. (ESV)

Do you find forgiveness an easy step to take?

WHAT ARE the obstacles you encounter on the path of forgiveness? List them below and commit these obstacles to God. He can dismantle strongholds of unforgiveness in your life.

SURVIVING THE STORMS OF LIFE

*he raging wind was forcing my trees to bend in submission to its power. The rain was hammering my shingles. My house groaned at the brute force of the storm. Thunder shook the skies and lighting flashed, slashing through the clouds. I was safe this time because I was in my home.

But how do I handle a storm of adversity? When there is no shelter and no relief?

I grasp my umbrella of praise, remembering all the times when God has been with me, even though in the midst of a storm, He can seem so distant.

My trench coat of intimacy with God shields my heart from the cold, brisk winds of those who do not know how to love. Those who can only see the failures and refuse to see my successful ventures.

Then I pull on my rain boots sloshing through the mud of the painful debris, knowing that on the other side is forgiveness. Forgiveness is not only my gift to those who create storms of chaos in my life, but a gift of comfort to my heart.

In reflection, I know there is a rainbow following some storms. I will lift my eyes to the sky, for if I cannot see a rainbow, maybe I can see the silver lining of a cloud, and God will tenderly give me wisdom as to the why of the storm.

Genesis 9:12-17

12-16 God continued, "This is the sign of the covenant I am making between me and you and everything living around you and everyone living after you. I'm putting my rainbow in the clouds, a sign of the covenant between me and the Earth. From now on, when I form a cloud over the Earth and the rainbow appears in the cloud, I'll remember my covenant between me and you and everything living, that never again will floodwaters destroy all life. When the rainbow appears in the cloud, I'll see it and remember the eternal covenant between God and everything living, every last living creature on Earth." (The Message)

HOW DO YOU HANDLE ADVERSITY?

Do you focus on the negative or ask God to give you understanding as to what He is working in the midst of the storm?

Do you seek the rainbow or the silver lining to the clouds of adversity?

ANGRY IS AN UGLY WORD

*D*id you ever notice when people are angry their face changes? They clench their jaws, their veins pop out and no matter how beautiful or handsome they are when not angry, ugly takes precedence when they are.

In Genesis 4, there is an account of Cain and Abel and apparently Cain had his "ugly" on because God said, "Why are you so angry?" Then He followed that with, "Why do you look so dejected?"

I think dejected may be God's way of saying ugly.

Then God lays out a plan for escaping ugly and returning to normalcy ,and He gives it straight up to Cain. "You will be accepted if you do what is right. But if you refuse to do what is right, then watch out!"

Okay, now let me break that down.

If you don't do what is right, you become angry and then you end up looking ugly.

If you choose to do what is right, you can be happy and remain beautiful.

I don't know about you, but I prefer beautiful.

Genesis 4:6-7 [6] *Then the LORD said to Cain, "Why are you angry? Why is your face downcast?* [7] *If you do what is right, will you not be accepted? But if you do not do what is right, sin is crouching at your door; it desires to have you, but you must rule over it." (NIV)*

Do you get angry when things don't go your way?

WHAT STEPS COULD you take to defer from anger and respond with grace instead?

THE PATH OF FORGIVENESS

I had dated the man for over four years. There were times throughout our relationship when I knew I loved him, but there were more times when we fought viciously with each other.

He was very generous with me and my children and said he wanted to marry me from our first date. I didn't know I even had feelings for him until we had dated for six months.

Finally, after four and a half years, I was fed up, and I basically tried to go no-contact with him.

He continued to pursue me. At first, he called me cold and heartless for breaking up with him. He asked me why I had broken up with him and wanted to talk to me.

Problem was, I had been talking to him for over four years about my issues with the relationship, and he hadn't listened. My thinking was, why would he listen now?

Then he said he had gotten close to God, and he had forgiven me. I bristled at the thought that he was using the "God" card.

Last week, someone put me in a bind, and I knew the only way I could get out of this bind was to contact this man. So, I did.

We had to meet. He said he wanted to tell me about his God experience.

I thought, "Yeah, I want to see if this is really a God experience or just another play for my emotions."

When we met to talk, he said one night as he was lying in bed and thinking of me, he heard the words, "Forgive her. Deep down in your heart, you need to forgive her."

He said, a dark cloud lifted from his soul at that very moment.

But that is not the most amazing thing. The most amazing thing is what God did next. He showed *him* all the times he had hurt or disrespected *me*.

He is a sweet soul, and he was mortified. He said he needed to confess a lot of this to me.

This experience leaves me in awe of God. When he asks you to forgive someone for what they have done to hurt you, I think it is totally awesome that the way he does that is to show you how you hurt them first.

Somehow, when we look in the mirror of truth, it becomes harder to throw stones at another person's glass house.

Ephesians 4:32 *32 Be kind and compassionate to one another, forgiving each other, just as in Christ, God forgave you. (NIV)*

WHEN YOU HOLD unforgiveness in your heart towards someone, do you examine how you may have hurt them?

Is your litmus test for forgiving others based on how much they hurt you, or is it based on the sacrifice of Jesus?

MEN OF GOD

A single mother needs a man who will have her back. One who will stand up for her and fight for her when other people are tearing her down.

She needs someone who esteems her above all others. Who respects her in front of her children and who does not tolerate them disrespecting her in his presence.

A single mother needs someone who will not seek to control her for his own benefit but will breathe life into her world. Someone who believes in her potential and nurtures her dreams to become what God has called her to be. She needs someone who is not an anchor for her boat but wind in her sails.

She doesn't need someone who tries to get her children's adoration to be directed toward him but deflects it to her, because she has done the work of raising her children.

A single mother needs someone whom she can confide in without fearing the pain being deepened by revealing her heart.

A single mother needs, if necessary, a man who can intimidate her ex-husband and instill fear into him so that even though he did not respect her in the marriage, from that point on, he had better not even *think* about disrespecting her again.

I have some wonderful men in my life who are my protectors. I find it interesting that they have *never* been the men that I have dated.

Although I did not date them, I couldn't ask for better friends and, without exception, they are all upstanding Christian brothers. I care for them with a deeper and purer love than any of the men I have called my "boyfriends."

I am thankful to God for these men who have stood beside me, had my back, and shared their wisdom with me when the devil was using others to try to destroy me.

If you know a single mother and you have a heart for God, I encourage you to be a man of God in her life.

James 1:27 Pure and genuine religion in the sight of God the Father means caring for orphans and widows in their distress and refusing to let the world corrupt you. (NLT)

How do you treat single parents, whether they are single mothers or single fathers?

If you are dating a single mother, do you treat her with honor and respect?

JUST ONE THING...

~~~~~~~~~~~~~~~~~~~~

*I*n the garden of Eden, everything was perfect, newly created by a magnificent and intelligent being called God. It left nothing to be desired. Adam and Eve had access to every tree for food and, although they were to tend the garden, it was not cursed, but blessed. Could you imagine a garden with no weeds or irritating insects? I think that may be what the Garden of Eden was like.

There was only one thing which was off limits. That one tree in the middle of the garden. That beautiful tree with delicious looking fruit. The tree of the knowledge of good and evil. This was the one thing which God had withheld as if to test their love and obedience. Eve had only to resist one thing, and she failed.

How the history of the world would have been changed if Eve had looked around her and been grateful for all that God had given her.

If she had enveloped her world with praise and gratitude she would still be in paradise. Instead, she focused on the one thing she couldn't have.

If you are single do you focus your time, energy and attention on the one thing you don't have, that being a spouse? Or do you inhabit the paradise of praise and give glory to God for all that you do have?

I have found when I respond with gratitude to what I have been

72

blessed with, it takes my focus off of the things or relationships I have not yet gained.

Genesis 3:2-3 [2] *The woman said to the serpent, "We may eat fruit from the trees in the garden,* [3] *but God did say, 'You must not eat fruit from the tree that is in the middle of the garden, and you must not touch it, or you will die.'" (NIV)*

If you are unmarried and desiring a spouse, how much time do you devote to yearning for this one desire to be quenched?

WHERE IS YOUR FOCUS?

WHY NOT ME?

Several of my friends have gotten bitten by the love bug. A few lucky ones have found their soulmates. I love these friends and I am grateful they have found true love.

Some of my casual friends have gotten married and divorced again within a short time. I can't imagine going through that trauma.

I have had several proposals for marriage. One even had a sparkling diamond in the mix, yet I declined all of them. I didn't think I would be happy in the long-term with these men and marriage, for me, is a long-term commitment.

The other day I reached out to another friend who had gotten bitten by the bug. I asked her if she liked the guy who had "set his cap for her." She responded in the affirmative. She had taken me aside on a previous occasion and literally gushed over him.

She has been through so much over the past few years, and I am really glad that she is finding love again, but I need to be honest. I didn't want to hear about it, cause it hadn't yet happened to me.

So, I called a dear friend who is single. This sweet young lady has never been married and has been praying for her husband since she was fifteen years old. She is now thirty-six. The Spirit of God has given both of us a promise of marriage. So, we talked, bellyached, and complained about God's timing.

Honestly, there was a significant time in my life I did not want to get married, but God instilled the desire through his promise, and I have submitted to His will.

I finished my walk and ended the call, feeling comforted by the conversation. I was walking down the hallway to my laundry room when I heard the words. "You're traveling."My mind stopped as if hit by a lightning bolt as I accepted the wisdom of those two words.

I have always wanted to travel. I love traveling. I find the adventure of traveling to be invigorating. For most of my adult life, I could only afford to travel within the states. Last year after Thanksgiving, I flew to Italy and had the time of my life.

Travel is something I can work into my budget and I do enjoy it. On most trips, I also promote or write, so I can work while vacationing. Traveling is an activity which I have yearned for all my life and I can do so now.

How do I respond?

Instead of rejoicing in that, I am complaining about my second husband not showing up.

I pivoted my thinking. I began thanking God for all the trips I took last year and there were many.

The gratefulness overflowed into thanking God for my occupation. Writing for Christ brings me so much joy and satisfaction. Although Christian writing has been a challenge financially, I am walking in faith and know God will provide.

I thanked him for my wonderful home, my car, my wardrobe, food in my fridge and freezer and my lovely Calico cat as well. I continued in my prayer of gratefulness, thanking him for the privilege of being able to babysit my grandson weekly, as well.

When I was reading my Bible this morning, I was reading about Jacob and Joseph. Joseph was a major figure in the Egyptian government, and his family was starving in Canaan. Jacob loved Joseph but had thought for twenty-two years that he had died.

Then a famine happened and Jacob's family was starving. The only country which had food was Egypt. Jacob asked his sons to go back to Egypt to get more food. Joseph's brothers were forced to get the food from Joseph. Soon the family was reunited.

If the famine had not happened, Jacob would have never seen his beloved son Joseph again.

Sometimes when we are in a famine, we focus on the famine. If we look only at the famine we may be unaware of the hidden blessings. Traveling is my blessing, and as I wait in expectation for more of God's blessings, I rejoice in what I have been given.

1 Thessalonians 5:18 Be thankful in all circumstances, for this is God's will for you who belong to Christ Jesus. (NLT)

Genesis 43:1 Now the famine was still severe in the land. ² So when they had eaten all the grain they had brought from Egypt, their father said to them, "Go back and buy us a little more food." (NIV)

When you are praying for something and you know it is God's will, but it is taking longer than you would like, are you open to unexpected blessings?

Do you focus on your wants and needs or what you can be grateful for? List ten items that you can thank God for.

YOUR CRISIS HAS BECOME YOUR CHRIST

*Y*ou would have thought the sky was falling down around me. My ex-husband went through a difficult time financially and was unable to provide child support. He didn't pay much to begin with, but I sincerely appreciated what he contributed to the children's welfare. He had always been very prompt with paying until this point.

When he stopped paying, I literally flipped out. I told everyone about it in my circle of friends and coworkers. I went on and on and had the "victim" role down pat. I am surprised anyone asked how I was doing because the moment they asked I went into a diatribe about my ex.

In addition, I was not kind to my ex. I should have been because he was a very present father when the children were young, but at this time he had moved to another state, and I resented that. As a result, my attitude was not good.

I was in the midst of this turmoil when I heard the counsel of God. In a gentle and nurturing tone, with a morsel of heart break, I heard, "Your crisis has become your Christ. You used to talk about me all the time and now all you talk about is your crisis."

I had to agree. I normally talk about God all the time, and this bump in the road had somehow become the topic of nearly every conversation I had.

I stopped that nonsense then and there and diverted my direction back to praising God.

It is so easy to give the platform over to negativity and, in essence, the devil when things don't go our way, isn't it? But how does that glorify God?

Colossians 3:17 And whatever you do, in word or deed, do everything in the name of the Lord Jesus, giving thanks to God the Father through Him. (ESV)

WHAT DO you focus on in conversation?

Do you glorify God in your conversations or provide a platform for your current crisis?

THE SOLITARY ACT OF LOVE

We begin this life as solitary creatures. We begin in a womb and return to dust.

Throughout our life we branch out as if we are a tree. The branches seek the sunshine of love and extend out to touch family and friends. Our roots dig deep for a belief system which can nurture our trunk and branches.

As life courses through us, we have a desire to unite with someone else. Someone whom we can trust and love in a special way. Someone who will become one with us within God's covenant of marriage. Two who become one are stronger than each on their own.

The devil does not favor this strength. Through deceit and betrayal, he rips the oneness apart to leave gaping wounds of emotional and spiritual pain. This is divorce.

So now one must be solitary again.

But alas, if you have God, you are never alone. You may feel alone, for it is hard to hug a Spirit.

In my novel, The Shattered Vase, Susie, the main character states this when she says, "It is difficult, at times, to love a God who is invisible."

Hope responds. "Is it easier for you to love a man who can leave you for another woman?"

Do you feel the love of God when you are in the midst of heartache?

As you look at life through the prism of eternity, the love of another is temporary. God's love is eternal and unconditional.

May you be wise in the love you choose.

1Corinthians 7: 7-9 Sometimes I wish everyone were single like me—a simpler life in many ways! But celibacy is not for everyone any more than marriage is. God gives the gift of the single life to some, the gift of the married life to others.

8-9 I do, though, tell the unmarried and widows that singleness might well be the best thing for them, as it has been for me. But if they can't manage their desires and emotions, they should by all means go ahead and get married. The difficulties of marriage are preferable by far to a sexually tortured life as a single. (The Message)

Do you rejoice in the simplicity of being single?

Can you list ten things that you can do while being single which you may have to forego if you were married?

ACKNOWLEDGMENTS

The primary reason why I write is because of the relevance and meaning God has so graciously given to my life. So, He gets the first offering of thanks for His magnificent love.

Then there are others...

I want to thank all of my friends who have been so supportive on my journey of writing. Doug, Judy, Debbie, Charlotte, Margaret, Janice, Dan, Carol, Wendy, Penny, Linda, Gloria, Gary, Peter, Robert, Lydia, Caroline and Tonya.

My family has been supportive as well. I appreciate the freedom they have granted me, even though becoming a self-published author is a road less traveled.

There are many more who have supported me. Each of you who purchased my first novel, The Shattered Vase, and my first children's book, The Holly and Bella Story, have touched my heart in a very special way. For those of you who have written reviews I am so very grateful.

I want to give special recognition to my friend, Tonya Matthews, who has edited this devotional, created my logo, and designed the cover for this book. Tonya, you are a blessing from God!

ABOUT THE AUTHOR

Gracie Lynne started her writing journey by writing a spiritual warfare novel. The Shattered Vase. This book was very well received and won an award and gained 5 star reviews.

After she released her second version of The Shattered Vase she released her first children's book. The Holly and Bella Story.

While Gracie was working on her first novel, she was also blogging. Many of her blogs involved lessons she learned through dating. She is happy to share these lessons with her readers through her devotional entitled, Just one…The Dilemma of Dating.

facebook.com/gracielynneauthor
instagram.com/gracielynneauthor

ALSO BY GRACIE LYNNE

The Shattered Vase

The Holly and Bella Story